America's Most Notorious Serial Killers: Biographies on Ted Bundy, Jeffrey Dahmer, and John Wayne Gacy (Killer Clown)

By: Jason Stonewall

Ted Bundy: A Biography

Introduction

Ted Bundy is one of the most infamous serial killers in American history and his life has been the subject of countless books and movies. His friendship with author Ann Rule was the theme of Rule's "The Stranger Beside Me." He confessed to murdering over 30 women between 1974 and 1978 in seven different states. The total number of murders Bundy committed remains unknown, but authorities believe he was responsible for over 100 murders. Throughout his life he was regarded as smart, handsome, and charismatic. His murders left countless women in America fearful that they could be his next victim. He was arrested and convicted of multiple murders and executed on January 24, 1989 at the Florida State Prison. He is now known as a sadistic, heartless, and evil sociopath that took immense pleasure in torturing, killing, and raping his victims. Members of Bundy's own criminal defense team believed he was born evil.

Early Life

Theodore Robert Cowell was born on November 24, 1946 to Eleanor Louise Cowell. Bundy's mother spent the last few months of her pregnancy at the Elizabeth Lund House for Unwed Mothers in Burlington, Vermont. Bundy's father was absent and Cowell struggled to support herself while pregnant with Bundy. Cowell claimed that Lloyd Marshall was Bundy's father. Marshall had served with the United States Air Force and worked as a salesman. Bundy never met Marshall. Cowell put Marshall's name as the father on Bundy's official birth certificate.

Several years later, Cowell claimed that Marshall was not Bundy's real father and that a sailor named Jack Worthington fathered Bundy. However, Cowell's claims that Worthington was the father were never substantiated, as no records of him exist in the Naval or Merchant Marine archives. Several family members believed that Cowell's biological father, Samuel Cowell, was Bundy's real father.

Cowell and Bundy moved to Philadelphia and lived with Cowell's parents, Samuel and Eleanor. Bundy's grandparents decided to raise Bundy as their own son to help their daughter escape the intense scrutiny and negative social stigma of being an unmarried mother. For three years, everyone was told that Bundy's grandparents were his actual biological parents. Family members and friends believed Samuel and Eleanor were Bundy's birth parents. Bundy believed that his mother was his older sister.

It is not known exactly how or when Bundy found out who his true mother was. Bundy personally made several claims throughout his life about how he discovered the truth about his birth parents. He told a girlfriend that his cousin called him a bastard and showed him his birth certificate to prove it. Bundy also told biographer Hugh Aynsesworth that he personally located his birth certificate. Ann Rule, who wrote about working with Bundy, believes that Bundy found out in 1969 when he received a copy of his birth certificate from the Department of Vital Records in Vermont.

Bundy's own accounts of his childhood are conflicting. He shared with Rule that he loved his grandparents, respected them, and they treated him well. However, in 1987 Bundy and several family members told Bundy's attorneys that Samuel Cowell was violent, abusive, and psychotic. They stated that Samuel regularly assaulted and emotionally abused his wife, that he attacked his sister in law for oversleeping and threw her down the staircase, that he was extremely racist and made hateful comments about minorities, including Jews, Italians, and Catholics. And that he enjoyed throwing neighborhood cats by their tails. Samuel Cowell also had a history of beating the family dog, hallucinating, having conversations with people who were not real, and having rage filled outbursts when Bundy's paternity was questioned. Bundy's grandmother was reserved, shy, and quiet. She occasionally received ECT therapy for depression, and towards the end of her life was unwilling to leave her home. She struggled with severe depression throughout her life.

In 1950, Cowell moved with Bundy to Tacoma, Washington to live with her cousins, Alan and Jane Scott. Cowell was convinced to move by several family members and she changed her name to Eleanor Louise Nelson. The next year, Bundy's mother attended a singles night event at Tacoma's First Methodist Church. She met a man named Jay Culpepper Bundy, who was a chef at a local hospital. Shortly after meeting, the two married. Eleanor and Ted took the last name Bundy. Bundy's mother and step father had four children together.

Bundy spent much of his time watching and babysitting his younger siblings and never bonded with his step-father. His step-father tried to bond and connect with Bundy, but Ted rejected him for not being intelligent and not having a high paying career.

There are varying descriptions of Bundy's time in middle school and high school. Although Bundy claimed that he voluntarily isolated himself from peers because he had a difficult time connecting with others, classmates claimed he was well liked. Bundy enjoyed skiing and often stole skiing equipment and forged and fabricated lift tickets. He claims he drank alcohol and wandered the streets at night hoping to see scantily clad women through uncovered windows. Bundy also stated that he enjoyed reading true crime novels and liked to read books about violent sex crimes. He preferred books that had illustrations and pictures of sexual violence, corpses, and brutally maimed bodies.

He attended Woodrow Wilson High School and graduated with good grades but was arrested twice while in high school for burglary and grand theft auto. The charges were expunged when he turned 18.

Early Adulthood

After graduating from high school, Bundy enrolled and attended classes at the University of Puget Sound in 1965. He completed a year and then transferred to the University of Washington in 1966 where he chose to study Chinese. The next year, he began dating a fellow student, Stephanie Brooks. He chose to withdraw from the University of Washington in 1968 and worked several different minimum wage jobs. He also volunteered for Nelson Rockefeller's presidential campaign in Seattle. Bundy attended the 1968 Republican National Committee Convention in Miami, Florida as a delegate for Rockefeller.

Bundy's girlfriend soon ended their relationship, which left Bundy completely devastated. He decided to travel to Colorado before spending time with family in Arkansas and Philadelphia. He studied for one semester at Temple University.

In 1969, Bundy returned to Washington and began dating Elizabeth Kloepfer, who worked as a secretary at the University of Washington School of Medicine. She was originally from Ogden, Utah, and had recently divorced her husband. In 1970 Bundy worked for Ped Line as a delivery driver. He then decided to re-enroll at the University of Washington and major in psychology. He graduated in 1972 as an honor roll student and was viewed favorably by his professors.

Bundy also worked for his school's work study program at Seattle's Suicide Hotline Crisis Center in 1971 with Ann Rule. Bundy worked one night a week. He stated that at least once a month, one of the callers would be in the middle of a suicide attempt, and his job was to keep the caller on the phone until police could trace the caller's location. Rule, who'd previously worked as a police officer and was working on becoming a true crime author, was his co-worker. Despite working together, Rule never noticed anything off or abnormal about Bundy.

In 1972, Bundy volunteered for Governor Danial Evans' reelection campaign. He recorded Evan's opponent, Albert Roselli's, stump speeches and returned the records to Evans staff. Evans staff analyzed the recordings and used them to help Evan's secure reelection. When Evans won the election, Bundy was hired as an assistant for Ross Davis, who was the Chairman of the Washington State Republican Party. Davis thought highly of Bundy, and noted that he was motivated, aggressive, and intelligent.

Bundy also took the Law School Admissions Test and applied to law school. Even though his scores were average, he was accepted to the University of Puget Sound and the University of Utah. Strong letters of recommendation from Governor Evans, Brown, and several Professor's from the University of Washington's Department of Psychology helped secure his admission offers.

Bundy enrolled as a law student at the University of Puget Sound in 1973, and started dating Stephanie Brooks, his ex-girlfriend. Brooks was shocked at Bundy's complete transformation and saw that he had a bright future in the legal and political field. Bundy continued to date his current girlfriend and hid their existences from each other.

Bundy and Brooks became serious and discussed marriage. Bundy stopped all communications with Brooks in 1974. When Brooks eventually was able to get a hold of Bundy, she asked why Bundy had stopped speaking with her. Bundy responded by saying "Stephanie, I have no idea what you mean." Bundy said that he simply wanted to prove he could marry Brooks if he wanted too. However, Brooks believed that Bundy did it to get back at her for breaking up with him several years before.

Bundy also started skipping classes as the University of Puget Sound School of Law, and by April, he stopped attending law school entirely. Around this time, several women started going missing in the Pacific Northwest region of the United States. Around the same time Bundy was working as an assistant director for the Seattle Crime Prevention Advisory Board. He published a pamphlet about rape prevention that was meant to protect women from violent sexual crimes.

Life of Crime

It remains unknown when Bundy committed his first murder or kidnapping. Bundy gave different accounts of when he started killing throughout his life. Bundy admitted to committing his first murder in 1974 but made conflicting claims. He disclosed to psychologist Art Norman that he had committed his first murder in 1969, killing two women in Atlantic City, New Jersey while he was visiting his family in Philadelphia. He also claimed he committed his first murder in Seattle in 1971 and implied to a homicide detective that he committed his first murder in 1972 in Seattle.

Several people, including Rule, believe that Bundy may have committed his first murder at 14. Rule believed that Bundy killed 8-year-old Ann Marie Burr in Washington in 1961, but Bundy adamantly denied any involvement in Burr's death. Rule only ever uncovered circumstantial evidence connecting Bundy to Burr's death.

Bundy spent time mastering the art of killing. Since DNA profiling was rarely used, Bundy specialized in ensuring he left no forensic evidence behind at his crime scenes. He took extensive measures to make sure he never left behind incriminating evidence.

Throughout 1974, women at colleges in Washington and Oregon began disappearing at a rate of roughly one woman per month. Police were dumbfounded and couldn't link their disappearances to a suspect. Most disappearances resulted in no evidence being left behind for investigators.

On January 4, 1974, Bundy committed his first known assault. He broke into 18-year-old Karen Sparks' basement level apartment. He ruthlessly assaulted her with a metal rod that he took from Sparks' bed frame. After beating Sparks, Bundy sexually assaulted her with the same metal rod. Sparks was in a coma for 10 days. She survived, but was left with permanent, life-long physical and mental disabilities.

Bundy committed his first known murder on February 1, 1974. He broke into Lynda Ann Healy's basement room. Haley was a student at the University of Washington and worked broadcasting local weather reports for skiers. Bundy knocked her unconscious, then dressed her in blue denim jeans and a white shirt and put her in his car. She was never seen or heard from again. Years later, a piece of Healy's skull was found at one of the remote wooded locations where Bundy dumped and buried his victim's corpses.

Local college women continued to disappear. Bundy would regularly pick up local college aged women who were hitchhiking near campus. He would wear a fake cast and ask his victims to help him get items into his car. Once they were in his car, he would knock them unconscious, rape them, and kill them. Burying the bodies up to several hundred miles away in remote, wooded locations. Occasionally, Bundy would decapitate his victims, take their heads to his apartment, and sleep with them. He viewed murder as more than just a crime of passion or lust and that physical possession of the remains was the "ultimate possession." Bundy also believed that the places where he disposed of his victims were sacred.

Within six months, six women were confirmed missing and multiple other women had reported that a man had attempted to lure them away from a crowd at Lake Sammamish State Park. Two more women, Janice Ann Ott and Denise Marie Naslund were soon reported missing, last seen at Lake Sammamish.

On March 12, 1974, Bundy abducted, raped, and murdered Donna Gail Mason, who was 19 years old. She was an undergraduate student at The Evergreen State College in Olympia, Washington. Her whereabouts were unknown after she left her campus dormitory to attend a local jazz concert.

Shortly after, on April 17, Susan Elaine Rancourt, a Central Washington State College student, went missing while walking back to her dormitory after an evening meeting with advisers. Within weeks of her disappearance, two more female students at Central Washington State College reported strange encounters to police. One woman stated that on the same night that Rancourt disappeared, a man who was wearing an arm sling approached her to ask her to help him get books into his brown or tan colored Volkswagen Beetle. A second woman described an identical encounter that occurred three days after Rancourt went missing.

On May 6, Roberta Kathleen Parks disappeared. She left her Oregon State University dormitory to meet friends for coffee and never arrived. Despite increased concern from police departments in Seattle and Portland, women continued to disappear at an alarming rate.

On June 1, Brenda Carol Ball, who was 22, went missing after she left the Flame Tavern in Burien, Washington. Witnesses stated that she was seen in the parking lot with a man with brown hair wearing an arm sling.

On June 11, University of Washington student Georgann Hawkins disappeared. She was last seen walking in a well-lit alleyway that ran between her sorority house and her boyfriend's dorm. The next morning, three detectives and a criminalist from the Seattle Police Department painstakingly crawled through the alleyway on their hands and knees in a failed attempt to find evidence. When the police published Hawkins' disappearance in the local area, several witnesses shared that they saw a man in the alley that night who was on crutches and attempting to carry a briefcase. One female witness stated that the man asked her to help him put the briefcase in his light brown Volkswagen Beetle.

The disappearances were widely publicized in Washington and Oregon, and women became extremely fearful of walking alone at night or hitchhiking. Most young women stopped hitchhiking entirely and significant pressure was placed upon law enforcement to identity and arrest the perpetrator.

Bundy was working full time with the Department of Emergency Services in Olympia during this time, and the organization was responsible for helping local law enforcement search for the missing women. Bundy also began dating Carole Ann Boone, his co-worker. She was a single mother with two kids, who had been through two divorces.

Police began noticing similarities between the victims. All the victims were white, young, attractive female college students who parted their hair down the center. All the disappearances occurred at night or in the early morning and near active construction zones. All the abductions occurred within one week of college midterms or final exams and sightings of a man wearing an arm sling or using crutches and driving a brown or tan Volkswagen Beetle occurred near all the crime scenes. All the women were also wearing slacks or denim jeans.

On July 14th, 1974, two women, Janie Ann Ott and Denise Marie Naslund, went missing after they left with a man while at Sammamish State Park. Ott was 23 and worked as a probation officer and case worker with the King County Juvenile Court. Naslund was 19 and was in school studying computer programming.

Five witnesses came forward with significant details. The witnesses shared that a young, attractive man wearing a white tennis outfit and a sling on his left arm, who spoke with a slight accent was asking for help disconnecting his sailboat from his brown Volkswagen Beetle. The man said his name was Ted and four different women refused to follow him to his car. One woman did, but upon seeing that there was no sailboat, ran.

Ott was seen following the man to his car after hearing his sailboat story. Naslund disappeared after going to the restroom. Police compiled a profile and sketch, opened a tip line, and shared the information with the public. Four different people - Elizabeth Kloepfler, Ann Rule, a DES co-worker, and a University of Washington Psychology Professor, all reported Bundy as a possible suspect to detectives. However, their tips were ignored. Detectives were receiving hundreds of different tips daily and didn't believe that Bundy, who had no adult criminal record and was a law school student, was a plausible suspect.

In September, two hunters found human remains two miles away from Sammamish State Park. After reporting their findings, it was discovered that the remains were Ott and

Naslund. However, additional skeletal remains, including femurs and vertebrae, were also uncovered. Six months later, several forestry students who were studying at Green River Community College found human skulls and jawbones on Taylor Mountain. The remains belonged to Healy, Rancourt, Parks, and Ball. Bundy frequently hiked the trails where the remains were found.

Bundy enrolled at the University of Utah School of Law in August 1974. He enrolled as a first-year student. While he wanted to succeed in school, he found that the classes were incomprehensible and he lacked the intellectual ability to master and understand the material. He found his inability to grasp law extremely disappointing. He maintained a long-distance relationship with Kloepfer, who remained in Seattle. He also continued to date other women.

In September, women started disappearing. Bundy raped and murdered an unknown hitchhiker in Idaho on September 2, 1974. It is unknown whether he immediately dumped the body in a nearby river or came back the next day to document and photograph the corpse and then dismember it. On October 2, 1974, Bundy abducted, raped, and murdered 16-year-old Nancy Wilcox in Holladay, Utah, which is a suburb near Salt Lake City. He took her to the woods and raped her. Bundy claimed that he planned on letting her go, but accidently strangled her to death trying to silence her screams for help. Bundy buried her remains 200 miles away at Capitol Reef National Park, but Wilcox's body was never found.

On October 18, Bundy kidnapped, raped, and murdered 17-year-old Melissa Anne Smith. She was the daughter of the Chief of Police of Midvale. She disappeared after she left a local pizza place. Her body was found 9 days later in a wooded, mountainous area, the corpse was naked.

On October 31, Laura Ann Aime disappeared after leaving a local coffee shop. She was 17 years old, her naked body was discovered in American Fork Canyon on Thanksgiving Day. Autopsy's on both Smith and Aime confirmed that both were assaulted, raped, sodomized, and strangled to death with a pair of nylon stockings.

On November 8, Bundy attempted to abduct Carol DaRonch, who was 18 and worked as a telephone operator. While in the parking lot at the Fashion Place Mall, Bundy identified himself as "Officer Roseland," stating he was a police officer at the Murray Police Department. He claimed that someone attempted to break in and steal DaRonch's car and that she needed to file an official police report. When DaRonch noticed that Bundy wasn't driving to the local police station, Bundy pulled over onto the side of the road and tried to handcuff her. Bundy accidently put both cuffs on the same wrist and DaRonch was able to escape.

That night, Debra Jean Kent, a 17-year-old student at Viewmont High School disappeared. She was last seen leaving a school play on the way to pick up her brother. Two witnesses, the high school's drama teacher and a student, told police that they spoke to a strange man who asked them to come out to the parking lot and help him identify a car. Other witnesses noticed a man matching the same description pacing outside in the parking lot. Detectives found a set of keys that unlocked the handcuffs on DaRonch's wrist while canvassing the school's parking lot.

Kloepfler, who was still dating Bundy, called the King County police in November upon hearing that local women were disappearing. She shared that she believed Bundy was the perpetrator, and participated in an extensive interview with Detective Randy Hergesheimer, who worked with the Department's Major Crimes Unit. Although Bundy remained a top suspect, witnesses from Lake Sammamish did not identify Bundy in a photo lineup. A month later, Kloepfler called the Salt Lake County Sherriff's Department and reasserted her belief that Bundy was behind the disappearances. The Sherriff's Department included Bundy on their list of suspects but didn't have any evidence connecting him to the crimes.

Bundy came back to Seattle in January 1975 for one week and spent most of his time with Kloepfler. Bundy also began committing his crimes further east in Colorado. He committed his first murder in Colorado on January 12, 1975. Caryn Eileen Campbell, who was a 23-year-old registered nurse, disappeared abruptly while she was walking back to her room at the Wildwood Inn. She was walking down a well-lit hallway at the time of her disappearance. She was last seen alive in Snowmass Village. Her body was discovered one month later on a remote, secluded dirt road near the resort. The autopsy concluded she died from blunt force head trauma and linear grooves were found depressed on her skull. Her body had multiple massive, deep cuts.

On March 15, Julie Cunningham, who was a 26-year-old ski instructor in Vail, was reported missing when she never arrived to meet her friend for dinner. Bundy stated that he lured Cunningham to his car by approaching her while he was on crutches and asked her to help him get his skis in his car. He then clubbed and handcuffed her and raped and killed her 90 miles away in Rifle, Colorado.

Several weeks later, Bundy raped and killed 25-year-old Denise Lynn Oliverson. He abducted her while she was riding her bike to her parent's house near the Utah-Colorado border. Oliverson was last seen alive on April 6, 1975.

Bundy kidnapped Lynette Dawn Culver from a middle school in Idaho on May 6. She was 12 years old. He killed her by drowning her and then proceeded to have sex with her corpse in his hotel room. He dumped her body in a nearby river.

Bundy's next victim, Susan Curtis, disappeared from the Brigham Young University campus on June 28. Several months later, Bundy was baptized at The Church of Jesus Christ of Latter Day Saints, but never became active in any church activities, worship, or functions. He also ignored most of the restrictions of the church involving alcohol use, pre-marital sex, and smoking.

Washington police were still attempting to solve the slew of murders Bundy committed in 1974. They used a payroll computer to create a database of all the information involving the deaths and disappearances that occurred in 1974. They included all the known information about the investigations, including the victims, their associates, the name Ted, a Volkswagen Beetle, and the final list of potential suspects included 26 different men. Investigators also made a list of the top 100 suspects. Ted Bundy was on both lists.

Arrest

The beginning of Bundy's downfall happened on August 16, 1975. A Utah Highway Patrol officer became suspicious when he saw Bundy driving around a neighborhood very early in the morning. Bundy immediately fled at a high rate of speed when he saw the police car. The officer pulled Bundy over and searched his vehicle when he noticed Bundy's passenger seat was folded up on the back seat. When the officer searched the vehicle, he found a crowbar, handcuffs, a ski mask, a panty hose ski mask, rope, an ice pick, and trash bags. Bundy tried explaining that the he used the ski mask for skiing, that he found the handcuffs in a dumpster, and everything else was easily explained away as common household items. The officer originally believed the items were in Bundy's vehicle for burglary purposes.

The officer believed that Bundy matched the description of the man who had attempted to kidnap DaRonch. Police searched Bundy's apartment. They found a guide book for local Colorado ski resorts with the Wildwood Inn check marked and a brochure advertising the play at Viewmont High School that was performed the night Kent went missing.

The police did not have sufficient evidence to arrest Bundy and released him. Salt Lake City police placed Bundy on 24-hour surveillance. Three detectives flew to Seattle to interview Kloepher, Bundy's current girlfriend. Kloepher explained that she found strange objects around her home and in Bundy's apartment, including crutches, plaster of Paris, surgical gloves, and a bag of women's clothing. She shared that Bundy was impoverished and that she believed that he acquired most of his expensive possessions by stealing them. Kloepher was also interviewed by Seattle homicide detectives and was told that Bundy was briefly engaged to Stephanie Brooks in December 1973.

In September 1975, Bundy sold his Volkswagen Beetle to a local teenager in Midvale. Police immediately impounded the vehicle and conducted an extensive search. They found hair strands from Campbell, Smith, and DaRonch. The FBI believed that it would be statistically impossible for all three women's hair to be found coincidentally in the same car, because the three women did not know each other.

Police put Bundy in a lineup on October 2, 1975, and DeRonch stated Bundy was the man who attempted to kidnap her. Likewise, witnesses from the high school where Kent was abducted stated Bundy was the stranger they saw in the parking lot.

Police charged Bundy with kidnapping and attempted criminal assault, and Bundy's parents paid his $15,000.00 bail. Bundy stayed with Kloepfler in Seattle, where police kept Bundy under constant surveillance in the hopes of gathering enough evidence to charge him.

Bundy stood trial for the DaRonch kidnapping and attempted assault on February 23, 1976. He waived his right to trial by jury and proceeded with a bench trial, as suggested by his attorney. After four days of testimony, Judge Stewart Hanson Jr. found Bundy guilty on both counts, and sentenced Bundy to one to fifteen years of imprisonment at Utah State Prison.

While serving his sentence, Bundy was found hiding in the bushes in the prison yard with maps, plane schedules, and a social security card. He was placed in solitary confinement for several weeks. In October 1976, he was charged in Colorado for the murder of Caryn Campbell. He eventually waived extradition and was transferred to Aspen in January 1977.

Bundy elected to pro se and represent himself in the murder trial. On June 7, 1977, he was transferred from the county jail to the courthouse for a preliminary hearing. Since he was serving as his own attorney, he did not have to wear handcuffs or shackles. While in the law library conducting research for his case, he escaped through a second story window. He severely sprained his ankle in the fall. He took off his outer layer of clothes and proceeded to hike south through the Aspen Mountains. He broke into several cabins and structures to procure food and supplies. He eventually stole a car from the Aspen Golf Course, drove back to Aspen, and was pulled over by police for driving erratically.

The case against him was extremely weak, and Bundy won several pre-trial motions that deemed most of the evidence was inadmissible. Despite the favorable odds, Bundy planned another escape. He procured a hacksaw and $500 cash and cut a hole in the ceiling of his cell where he was able to access a crawlspace. On December 30, 1977, he climbed into the crawlspace, broke into the warden's apartment, changed into street clothes, and walked out of the jail. He stole a car which broke down on Interstate 70. A nearby motorist gave him a ride to Vail, where he took a bus to Denver and then caught a flight to Chicago. His escape was discovered 17 hours later. He then took a train to Ann Arbor, Michigan, and from there stole a car and drove to Atlanta, Georgia. He took a bus to Tallahassee, Florida, and rented a room in a boarding house. He believed he could remain undetected if he resisted criminal activity but was unable to obtain a job because he didn't have any identification.

On January 15, 1978, he broke in to the Chi Omega sorority at Florida State University. He proceeded to attack four women. He beat 21-year-old Margaret Bowman with a piece of firewood, sexually assaulted and beat 20-year-old Lisa Levy, assaulted Kathy Kliener, breaking her jaw, and finally attacked Karen Chandler. All four assaults were done within 15 minutes. He then proceeded to attack FSU student Cheryl Thomas, and his assault left her permanently deaf. On her bed, they found semen and two hairs that resembled Bundy's. On February 9, he unsuccessfully attempted to abduct 14-year-old Leslie Parmenter. Later that day he kidnapped and murdered 12-year-old Kimberly Leach from her middle school. Leach's remains were found mummified at a pig farrowing shed 35 miles away.

On February 15, Bundy was arrested in Pensacola when an officer pulled him over because the car Bundy was driving was reported stolen. He had 21 credit cards and the FSU identification cards of several of his victims. After attempting to flee, Bundy was subdued. Bundy was charged with the murder of Levy, Bowman, and Leach, as well as the assaults on the other Chi Omega sorority women. He rejected an offer by the prosecution to plead guilty and receive a 75-year sentence.

His trial was the first to ever be televised in the United States. Although he had 5 court appointed attorney's, he handled much of his own defense. He was found guilty on July 24, 1979 of murdering Bowman and Levy, and for the attempted murder of Kleiner, Chandler, and Thomas. He was found guilty six months later for the murder of Leach. He was sentenced to death in both cases. After a series of failed appeals, Bundy was executed on January 24, 1989.

Jeffrey Dahmer: A Biography

Introduction

The name Jeffrey Dahmer probably conjures up all sorts of distorted images in one's mind. The man is known as one of the most notorious serial killers in history. Perhaps the reason for his infamy centers around how relatively recent he was in circulation, committing his heinous crimes for his own perverse pleasure. And because as human beings we rubber neck at train wrecks and are sometimes ironically drawn to wicked deeds from the comfort of our homes, observing characters from a distance is often too tempting to pass up. We read stories of Charles Manson or Ted Bundy with mixed feelings of disgust and curiosity, wondering how someone could have done such atrocious things. We dole out ethical judgements on the perpetrators. And often, the true crime genre is structured in a way that is very fun to read, like a thriller set in real life, educational and entertaining, but very terrifying due to the implication that what is being read has truly happened and isn't the product of a Hollywood script. Regardless, there is considerable importance in the study of and interest in, social deviants. Attempting to understand them is a step in the right direction for preventing as many Dahmer-like occurrences as humanly possible. But just as human behavior is erratic and the nature of preventing crime is very sci-fi in scope, we have to accept that the world is entropic enough to warrant deviations of the norm. Horrors will occasionally happen. We shouldn't avert our eyes, but face them bravely. This isn't to desensitize ourselves, but to further entrench ourselves in an empathetic connection with the victims and to further diagnose how to prevent the next Dahmer from committing similar crimes. To further understand the man, let's dive into the details of his life that lead up to crime. Then, we will discuss the crimes themselves, all the way to his conviction and death.

Dahmer's Younger Years

Dahmer's parents were Lionel Herbert Dahmer and Joyce Flint. Born in Milwaukee, Wisconsin, the two weren't the most compatible, but they wasted no time in having a son. Lionel and Joyce were polar opposites, the former being an academic chemist with hardly an emotive bone in his body, while the latter was emotionally-driven and wanted to be the apple of almost everyone's eye. Different upbringings and personality types lead to common gaps between people; why the two decided to tie the knot and have kids is more mysterious than your average recitation of "opposites attract." Common sense would tell you that there seems to be a cutoff in the amount of opposition that a couple can hope to operate healthily under, but love often doesn't make sense. In short, the two were a very strange choice for lovebirds, but regardless, Joyce became pregnant "within days of their marriage."

The birth of Jeffrey Lionel Dahmer on May 21, 1960 filled both parents with joy. Their incompatibility was washed away through the joys of parenthood. He was a weak baby at first, requiring casts and lifts on his shoes until he was six years old, but Jeffrey Dahmer passed every other test with flying colors. "All in all, it was the unremarkable advance of a pretty healthy, normal baby, with every promise of a happy childhood ahead of him." And he had a pretty normal childhood indeed, filled with pets and adventures, but there was one constant in his life that may have contributed to an aberration in his psychological development: his parents bickered and he felt distanced from them. Some would theorize that even his mother's decision to stop breastfeeding him because he wasn't cooperating as he should have been as an infant, might have contributed to feelings of rejection much too young for Jeffrey. The details and circumstances are probably much too complicated to pinpoint any one occurrence. And plus, who's to say that the brunt of the blame should be given to environmental factors over a deep-seated genetic causality. Regardless, Dahmer didn't have the healthiest of familial relations, but in all honesty, how many people really do have the most ideal upbringing? A lot less than is probably reported.

Continuing the subject of the influential factors in Jeffrey's early life, Lionel Dahmer moved his family closer to Marquette University, so that the patriarch of the family could study for his Master's degree in Analytical Chemistry. This move was met with a lot of resistance by Joyce, who declared "the neighbors, once again, irksome. Noise of any intensity distressed her out of all proportion, especially if it was made by other people." After Lionel obtained his degree, the family packed up again and moved to Iowa, so that he could continue his post-grad work at Iowa State. The move to the more nature-oriented Iowa was a delight for the young Jeffrey as he was very excited to be around Iowa fauna. But this was only a consolation prize of his move.

For it was in Iowa that he was first enrolled in school (nursery school). Through his time there, he was shown to not really fit in or belong with the other kids. He was shy, timid, and awkward. And, "because he was called 'new boy' all the time, he imagined that such was his adopted name in these strange surroundings." He just didn't take to school at all and he was not helped much in assimilating and becoming a healthy functioning member of his new social environment. And to top off the stress of not fitting in with his peers in school nor having any significant encouragement or help to integrate himself socially, he was faced with a really serious operation regarding hernias he had developed.

His double hernia surgery was performed on March 19, 1964. He was only four years old at the time and Masters says in his book The Shrine of Jeffrey Dahmer, that the operation would have been tough on a fully-developed adult. To face such an operation at the age of four might have caused him trauma, also considering that when talking about the surgery years later he disclosed that he had thought his genitals had been removed. The pain was that bad. Masters then brings up a good point that "one may well wonder, in view of the boy's later disturbance and the florid nature of its manifestation, whether this operation was perhaps disproportionately significant in his life." With that operation marking the inception of his childhood though, Dahmer by his own assessment had a pretty normal childhood. From an objective standpoint, he was a shy boy and continued to be well into his later years. But he did have some regular friends he played with around the neighborhood and like any young boy, he got into trouble. Despite the normalcy though, he was perhaps a little too interested in animals. With what we now know about Dahmer, it is easy to frame the narrative around his fascination and think that perhaps his interest in animals was always distorted. But like so many other kids, he was an animal lover.

There was a radiation testing facility on the fringe of Ames, Iowa, "where all kinds of barnyard animals were kept for study, and Jeff would often spend time in there watching and staring." Spending a lot of time here, his curiosity eventually got the better of him and he went forwards to sneak a peek. In an abandoned building, he pushed open the unlocked door and stepped inside to see the entire floor and stairs of the place was covered in rats and mice. He ran like the wind out of there. This illustrates just how vivid the memories of his childhood interactions with animals were: "his fascination with animals and insects grew unabated. Snakes, toads, crabs, turtles, fish, wild rabbits, and a kitten called Buff fed his curiosity and imagination." He found animal bones in the crawlspace underneath his house and his desire to know more about the inner workings of each animal grew more and more prominent.

Alongside these details comes the knowledge that Joyce Dahmer's mental health was declining considerably: "she began to take pills to calm herself down, and doubled the dosage when they failed to give her the peace she desired...Joyce was progressively becoming a desperate woman, and her consumption of medication would increase alarmingly over the next few years." It also didn't help that her husband was too busy with his professional life to give her the love and attention she needed, and she was underappreciated. This sent her into an even deeper funk. Perhaps, if Lionel Dahmer had placed more of an emphasis on her wellbeing then the Dahmer family dynamic wouldn't have been as unhealthy as it would come to be, but that's hard to definitively say. It is also true that Lionel did a lot of the shopping, helped with the household, and was constantly busy with his Doctorate work—a lot of blame can't be piled upon him. Sometimes, relationships just go bad.

The family moved to Ohio after Lionel earned his Doctorate and he and Joyce had another son. Jeffrey now had a little brother.

He had a new pet dog named Frisky as well, as a consolation for having to move and leave behind all of his other pets. At this time, Jeffrey was happy to have a younger brother, but he was also starting to withdraw a lot more. Masters says this about the traits he inherited from both of his parents: "Like his mother, he was dangerously self-centered; like his father, he was unnaturally reticent. He became silent and broody as a result." According to Masters again, Jeffrey exhibited traits common to a schizoid personality—the lack of trust among peers and his choice to isolate himself from all social interaction. They moved once more to a more stable location in 4480 West Bath Road in 1968. They would stay there for ten years, which for the Dahmer household was an eternity, relatively speaking.

The Bath Road House

As Masters says, the "Bath Road house was enchantment itself after the various makeshift homes the family had recently occupied. It was truly rural, surrounded by nature and air and peace." This would be paradise for the young Jeffrey. The junior high boy would spend the majority of his time alone, with secret pursuits. When he was with others or forced to do anything, he displayed a listless and lethargic attitude. He seemed most energetic when he was by himself, even if the things he found himself doing were of no singular importance. Lionel started to grow concerned for the wellbeing of the boy, thinking that he needed to act quickly or else he would continue to grow in his listlessness. But little did his father know that the young boy, although externally displaying signs of having a lackadaisical outlook on life, was actually pretty passionate about prehistory, science, geology, mycology, etc. Jeff and one of his friends actually participated in the science fair in their junior high. Dahmer began to feel comfortable enough to allow his friend David Borsvold into his private life a little bit. But that was only for a short moment. Dahmer still went off into the woods by himself and investigated the bones of animals, equating some of the fleshless animals with himself—he felt himself to be a shallow, lifeless husk of a person who didn't much belong with the rest of the world. This would only keep mushrooming to become far more serious. And the environs of the Bath Road house were definitely easy to get lost in for hours of solitude. In addition, he felt the need to get away from his mother by being by himself. It has been said that he blamed her depression and mental illness on himself; because he felt himself to be a burden to her, it was much easier to take himself out of the equation and enjoy his own company instead.

This does not mean that Lionel didn't try and get his son engaged like other normal boys through sports and other activities. "Lionel tried everything to engage his attention, awaken his energy. He taught him tennis, and played many a match with him. But Jeff's heart was not in the game." He played reluctantly, as if he was forced to. He was also made to join the Boy Scouts and even though he liked the outdoors and wildlife, he was unresponsive during the retreats that happened. His brother also chimed in on just how unresponsive and flat his voice was all throughout his childhood. Both he and his mother would shut off and become absorbed in their own little reality, separate from the normal realm of existence.

As Masters continues to touch on in The Shrine of Jeffrey Dahmer by page 54, Jeffrey started to change by the time he started high school. He also started to drink alcohol heavily. The reasons for his imbibing of alcohol are not exactly clear, but speculation centers on the idea that he may have been having a hard time existing in his own headspace without anyone in the world to call a friend. The alcohol definitely numbed his existence in a subjectively positive way, but physically it was very destructive. Dahmer also started acting socially bizarre. He took on the persona of a "class clown" type figure who would "bleat like a sheep in class and upset the equilibrium of discipline. Or he would fake an epileptic fit, or trip over an invisible object, or spit out his food and pretend to be sick." Masters expresses that Dahmer was merely inventing another character in order to further disguise the real Dahmer from everyone else. He was playacting in a rather heavy-handed way. But once he was on his own, he began sinking back into his real personality.

David, his brother, remembered the animal graveyard in the backward, near the small hut that Jeff had taken over for his own use: "Beside the hut was a small graveyard dedicated to the burial of animals, with small crosses and real animal skulls hanging from the crosses." To accompany this factoid, David also relates how Jeff wanted to show his little brother some of the things he was learning in his biology class and "produced a dead mole. He preceded to cut the mole open and remove the heart and liver which he then put in formaldehyde." Call it a morbid curiosity with biology that maybe gave his brother pause in retrospect. But in truth, no one really thought much of his behavior with animals: the dissections, skulls, obsessions, etc. "On the contrary, they appeared at last to indicate a proper interest in something, which could be nurtured and encouraged." His interest was showing that the boy had some life in him. Sure, his habits were a little strange, but at least he was doing something with his time.

Of course, his interest would morph into something else entirely: "He was starting to look out for 'road-kills,' animals which had collided with cars on the wide country highways, and bring them home. He did this several times over the next two years, cutting them open down the front to see what they looked like inside." Masters states that he never did kill any animals to inspect their insides; it was always already-dead animals his dissection tools were turned to. In a way he was like Leonardo Da Vinci—who was obsessed with anatomy and dissecting cadavers—with his desire to probe and find out the inner workings of each animal; but, that's where the comparisons stop between the two. And much like comparisons that aren't consistent in any major way, so to, Dahmer was different in psychological makeup from most young boys who grow up playing with dead animals. That is, Dahmer never tortured nor inflicted pain on another animal for sadistic pleasure. He was compassionate and gentle with animals. His fascination only extended towards the corpses of the animals and what was inside of them: "This obsession with the machine of life in preference to life itself is typical of the necrophile. " And so his obsession with vivisection continued to morph and evolve into what it would later become. But before that, so too his addictions and psychological afflictions would continue to bloom in a negative light.

When he was sixteen, Dahmer became friends with another student named Jeff Six, he was "one of Revere High School's suppliers of marijuana." This correspondence, coupled with Dahmer's alcoholism, was probably not the best relationship to spark, but both were in the same mental league and understood each other enough to get along. Masters says that "this new friendship suited Dahmer well enough because it involved neither emotional commitment nor contact with the real world. The dope and the alcohol were a passport to unreflective bliss." In addition to these vices that let him step outside of his mind and chemically bombard his nerve endings, he was starting to harbor strong sexual fantasies for men. Just a teenager of seventeen—without any sexual experience or anyone giving him that sort of attention—he was quickly learning to detach any sentiment from sexual acts. He would excessively masturbate, but like an immature individual not yet experienced in sharing a sexual experience unselfishly, his mentality was self-serving—the go-to methodology being to objectify the men he gazed upon in whatever magazine he was using. This, Masters says, was the beginning of his perverse objectification of people. Eventually both would meld together, the dead body and the sexual act, but they started off separate facets of learned behavior. Tragically, there was no one in his life that was aware enough to try and correct the fatal habits he was learning.

Dahmer's First Crime

The first homicide that Jeffrey committed was of Steven Hicks. Once Dahmer picked up Hicks as a hitchhiker, he invited him over for some beers. Steven acquiesced after some coaxing and they both hung out in Jeff's bedroom. Wanting to make a sexual move on his new acquaintance, Dahmer ultimately hesitated, learning soon that Hicks wasn't homosexual. Hicks kept talking about his girlfriend and how he couldn't wait to visit her. Masters says it like this, injecting a bit of speculation into the mix, but centering on a common anxiety that was a known issue in Dahmer's life—one that his father had worried about and would continue to worry about with his son: Dahmer started to become anxious because Hicks was talking about his future, all the plans he had, the exciting things he was going to do, and Dahmer had nothing planned. He was all alone, in his room, with no one to care for him. He was too afraid to make a move on Steven lest he would be rejected and left alone again. Non-sexual company was better than nothing at all, of course. But there was an insurmountable urge to act, to prevent Steven Hicks from leaving once he had sipped beers for a few hours. As Masters provides the inner monologue, "frustration within Jeff Dahmer rose until it filled his nostrils and pressed at his temples. He was not going to leave. He couldn't leave. He wouldn't let him leave."

As reactionary as anyone can be, Dahmer went below to the cellar, grabbed a barbell and struck Hicks dead. It was in a rush of excitement and terror-inducing emptiness of the mind that he did the act. He studied the boy before him, admired his work, and then promptly lost his mind with fear, unsure of what he had done and what he was going to do to cover it up. Having enough presence of mind to act, he grabbed the body and dragged it under the house, into the crawlspace where it laid all night. The next day, he went to the crawlspace and went about cutting the body into pieces as a means for transporting it easily to another location. Luckily for Dahmer, "at 4480 West Bath Road, a man could stand upright in the open end of the crawlspace." There was plenty of room to do the necessary work. During this time, he also had the chance to satisfy his curiosity like he had done with the animals, studying the inner machinery.

After this, he put the body into separate garbage bags and waited until three in the morning to head to a ravine where he was planning on dumping the body. Dahmer had to down a few drinks to muster up the courage for what he was about to do. What he didn't take into consideration was just how bad his driving would get being in such an inebriated state. He was pulled over by a police officer with Steven Hicks in his backseat inside the garage bags. He did the drunk driving protocol, passed the tests that were set up, was questioned on what he was doing out so late, and what the bad smell coming from the inside of his car was? Dahmer essentially said he was going to the city dump with trash, that "his parents were in the throes of a divorce and he couldn't sleep; he thought the drive would get things off his mind." It worked. The police officer let him go and regretted it immensely down the road when he realized and remembered that he had stopped Dahmer. As Masters says, "the Dahmer odyssey would never have occurred, and there would have simply been one more murder case in the local press to shake one's head over." Instead though, the bleak reality is that Dahmer would make it home, discard the body in a drainpipe, keep the head in his room for safekeeping for a few nights, and continue his perverse journey. He was just beginning.

Aimless Years, Life with His Grandma, and a Relapse

After some fruitless time at college where he stole from his roommates, drank most of the day, and flunked out, Dahmer enlisted in the army where he detoxed from alcohol, but quickly relapsed. Like school, he wasn't popular with his fellow soldiers and was actually physically beaten by a group of them who were tired of his constant insubordination which got them all in trouble collectively. After the army, he found himself back at home with his father Lionel and his new wife. His first order of business was to dig up the body of Steven Hicks and scatter the bones in the woods. It was a way of literally cleaning out the skeleton that had been overwhelmingly in his head for three years. It was after he did this that he felt like he could move on for a short period of time.

But, Jeffrey wasn't the most welcome addition to the house. Lionel Dahmer had gotten used to his new life and it was a much more peaceful dynamic than his marriage with Joyce. His new wife Shari was gainfully employed and wasn't neurotic. The twenty-one year old Jeffrey was a thorn in his father's side. He didn't have a job and was soon arrested for his drinking at a local Ramada Inn, so both Lionel and Shari came up with the idea to send him to live with his Grandma in West Allis, "to the house where Lionel himself had grown up and lived until his first marriage." The plan was that Dahmer would help her around the house and keep her company and he would have a place to stay. He shrugged and suddenly found himself living with his grandmother.

As agreed, he helped her with her chores and also managed to land himself a job as a phlebotomist shortly after moving to Wisconsin. He was fired after ten months, arrested for public urination at a state fair, and then he told himself that he was determined to "walk the straight and narrow" path in order to make himself right again. Whatever had gone wrong in his life he was now determined to fix. He had his church-going grandma to help him on this quest. And with her influence and his resolve, he managed two years where no incidents or scrapes with the law happened. Until one afternoon at the public library where he was sexually propositioned. Having never been in this situation before, the temptation for the "sexually untried" twenty-five year old Dahmer was too much to overcome. It caught him off guard as it would have likely caught anyone off guard to receive a note that requested their presence in a bathroom on the second floor of the library. He didn't go to meet the man who had left the note, but it triggered the feelings that he had fought so hard to suppress. And it was only a matter of time before he would become overwhelmed again.

He killed again, after two long years of fighting his inner demons, Dahmer erased his good streak at the age of twenty five. Many years after having killed Steven Hicks, by this time Dahmer's fantasies and sexual obsessions had grown so out of control that his only remedy was to give in. This was the case when Dahmer woke up one morning after having bedded a man named Steven Toumi in a room in the Ambassador Hotel. Dahmer woke up on top of him and he "immediately saw that the man was dead." His victim's bones were broken and caved in around his chest and ribs. Dahmer himself expressed shock and couldn't believe what he had done. He tried to remember what had happened or even committing the crime in the first place and he couldn't. He remembered that they both had been drinking rum, but there was no sign of the bottle or anything. Other crimes would follow. He said that "after the fear and the terror of what I'd done had left, which took about a month or two, I started it all over again. From then on it was a craving, a hunger, I don't know how to describe it, a compulsion, and I just kept doing it, doing it and doing it."

It happened again with James Doxtator, whom Dahmer invited back to his Grandmas house to stay the night. He offered James $50 to accompany him. And then he struck again, some hours later, after James expressed an interest to leave because he didn't want to stay out too late. The abandonment rubbed Dahmer the wrong way and he mixed James a drink with sleeping pills in them. He strangled him and kept the body around for five days until his Grandma began to notice and remark on the smell. And then after this it was Richard Guerrero. When the same methodology followed, he too became a victim. Sunday mornings, while his grandma was gone at church, became the most convenient time for him to get rid of the bodies of his victims. And that was that. He had a pattern now where he went to the Phoenix bar, invited men back to his Grandma's house, paid them $50, had sex, and then he mixed them the sleeping pill concoction before he strangled them. This would continue until the fortunate date that Dahmer was found out, many years later, when he had a place of his own and was a more seasoned veteran of killing.

Tracy Edwards Saves the Day

On July 22, 1991, Tracy Edwards, "who had a handcuff dangling from his left wrist," flagged down some police officers and told them that a guy had handcuffed him and he just wanted to get it off his wrist. They couldn't get the handcuffs off, so they had Tracy lead them back to Dahmer's residence at 924 North 25th Street. They went inside and Dahmer was very accommodating to the police officers, almost as if he didn't realize he should be acting nervous or afraid that officers of the law were in his killing house. He confirmed that he had put the handcuffs on Edwards and told the officer to get the key, it was in the bedroom. And it was in there that Mueller, one of the police officers, saw "that the top drawer of a chest was open, revealing pictures of scores of naked men. He looked further and realized, with some shock, that many of them were pictures of severed heads, dismembered limbs, decomposing torsos, and from the evidence of the décor in the pictures, it was clear that they were not commercially produced fakes." They restrained Dahmer and the searchn of his flat was underway. What they found was very disturbing. They opened the fridge and found the severed head of a black man and various other body parts that he was preserving.

Once he was detained, Dahmer disclosed everything in a cathartic rush. He wanted to set the record straight and tell all. He said that he had killed sixteen men in Milwaukee over four years; "that he had decapitated them, dismembered them, defleshed them and thrown what was left into the garbage; that some of the skulls he had retained." And so on and so forth until he had recounted the tale of his first murder of Steven Hicks, the murders in his Grandma's home, all the way to the time that Tracy Edwards had escaped Dahmer in one piece. Everything was catalogued and used as evidence. There were body parts, blood stains, tools, pornography, photographs, and the cops who interviewed Dahmer realized that everything he had told them was true and that he hadn't been feeding them half-baked information. He wasn't some "grandiose attention-seeking half-wit," but instead was telling the truth. After he was convicted, Dahmer didn't last long in prison. An inmate named Christopher Scarver ended up beating Jeffrey to death at the Columbia Correctional Institution where he was to live out his multiple life sentences. He died on November 28, 1994.

John Wayne Gacy: A Biography

Introduction

This is about John Wayne Gacy. The man has injected himself into the nightmares of the common people ever since he committed the crimes that would make him famous in the worst possible way. The atrocious and gruesome acts he committed have cemented his perverse legacy into the annals of serial killer history. He shares the same sort of reputation as Jeffery Dahmer, The Son of Sam, H.H. Holmes, Ted Bundy, the Zodiac Killer, and the Golden State Killer. Yet, by most who knew him personally, he was seen as a decent person. In the introduction of his book, The Man Who Killed Boys, Clifford Linedecker juxtaposes Gacy with two tragic and contemporaneous events that would frame the time period. Kennedy's assassination and the Jonestown massacre that happened under the supervision of Reverend Jim Jones. His arrest, after having molested and killed thirty-three young boys and buried them under his house, was equally as tragic and sinister in scope as the other events. And through the slayings the perpetuation of clown-phobias, fascination with the abnormal psychological ailments of the perpetrator, and the downright scariness of the event have lived on. Or, as Linedecker say: "The incidents capture our attention for a while until some new horror occurs to eclipse the old."

But reading and writing about the perverse and mysterious figure offers up opportunities to probe deeper and learn the motives of why someone would want to do something so horrible. Just like studying history to hopefully never repeat the more detrimental episodes of our humanity is helpful, so to, studying and trying to get inside an abnormal mind can provide insight into the causality of the crimes. As always, to understand on a more profound level, we should start with the childhood of the man in question.

The Childhood and Upbringing of John Wayne Gacy

Gacy was born on Saint Patrick's Day, 1942. At that time, as Linedecker states, those in Chicago (the entire nation as well) had been preoccupied with the Second World War. But, as a comparable characteristic to accompany the birth of someone who would grow to be a very violent man, Chicago was at that time "more known for the violent and venal ways of its citizens than for its positive accomplishments." Indeed, Chicago had a unique history with violence, perhaps only beaten by New York, as far as U.S. cities went. Al Capone, The Saint Valentines Massacre, Democratic Convention riots, and the Haymarket Riot, to name a few. And of course, during the World's Columbian Exposition, H.H. Holmes was murdering and "laying claim to the very unprosaic title of most industrious mass murderer in the history of the United States." The point being that Chicago had a reputation for harboring some very famous killers—this is obviously more statistically probable because the population of Chicago outranks many combined geographical areas in the nation. But regardless, as a framing device for the birth and upbringing of Gacy, he certainly fit in with Chicago's most violent offenders.

Gacy's father was a machinist whose name was John Wayne Gacy Sr. Young Junior was a decent student and lived in a respectable, clean household. They moved around as a family a few times in the Chicago area, but the boy never really gave a cause for concern through his behavior: "he was a typical neighborhood boy who joined the Boy Scouts, romped with his dog, and played stickball and other street games with his friends." Despite a few incidents—a blood clot in the brain caused by a concussive head injury—he was in good health for his age. In short, his life was so ordinary, as was his temperament and personality, as to not show signs of any deviation from the norm. Sometimes the predictive nature of childhood behaviors falls well short of any effective mark. The most stress that was caused during his childhood had to be the result of his having to move around and switch schools. He never did finish high school, and his interests, motivation, and focus always shifted with the constant musical chairs he and his family played. It certainly didn't contribute to a healthy state of feeling grounded in life.

Eventually, with a less than perfect relationship forming between him and his father, John Wayne Gacy felt the compulsion to leave his home while he was still just a teenager. He found himself in Las Vegas, but as is customary for those who have just arrived in Sin City, "newcomers are appreciated more if they arrive with money than without." And Gacy was left reeling with the tough reality that he was an inexperienced teenager without a diploma and needed to find work fast or else he was going to go hungry. He eventually found work as a custodian. Realizing his hasty mistake of heading to Las Vegas on a whim without so much as a plan, his new goal was to make enough money to get back home. And months later, he made enough and was "at home with his family, being fussed over by his sisters and eating his mother's cooking." After enrolling in Business College, he graduated. Things were looking up for the young man; there was not as much as a blip on the radar that would contribute to any lasting worry to an outside viewer. He was starting to get physically unhealthy though, but that paled in comparison to the prospects of his future that waited on the horizon.

He was going to be a salesman. Being equipped with a business degree and the loquaciousness of a natural businessman, his silver-tongued ways would pave the path of his career. Linedecker describes him as such: "He loved to talk. Words spilled topsy-turvy from his mouth, and few people listened closely enough to realize how little meaning the motley collection of words and phrases often had. He was articulate and ingratiating." After putting his natural talents to work, he quickly made a reputation for himself by being transferred to Springfield, Illinois where he managed a men's clothing store, Robert's Brothers. Not bad for a twenty-two year old. He held a degree in accounting and business management and was very active in Catholic clubs, he was also an officer of the Holy Name Society. In all, Gacy was a few marks shy of an upstanding citizen. What events or details or neurochemical aberrations could have led to the choices that he would later make?

Marriage and Legal Issues

In September 1964, he wasted no time in finding himself a wife. As Linedecker states, "he'd worked there only a few months before he had met, courted, charmed and—in September 1964—married a pretty co-worker, Marlynn Myers, in a Catholic Church ceremony." In today's parlance, she was out of his league in the looks department, but he made up for his physical limitations with his personality and charm. His ability to charm and persuade would provide a few key details about the tools he would use for his own sinister purposes. And if he was incapable of feeling empathy or he was in complete control of his ability to manipulate other people, he definitely showed it through his keen sales abilities and the charismatic aura he cast around him. Linedecker says that his wife watched him with wide eyes, marveling at how confident and adept he was at selling shoes and managing the retail business. And it was in Springfield that he was given a lot of opportunity to grow and develop as a young businessman, particularly when he joined the Junior Chamber of Commerce and was among young, ambitious people looking to make their community a better place. He started building his reputation through the work that he did with the "Jaycees." And his wife's parents had bought a few Kentucky Fried Chicken locations and were raking in some cash. Everything was copacetic for the Gacy's. Again, what went wrong? The answer to this question might hinge on his divorce from Marlynn years later. Or it might be something entirely different—a complicated array of happenings that all contributed to the skewed profile of Gacy. But things certainly started going south in his personal life relatively shortly.

Later, the Gacy family moved to Waterloo, Iowa as John's father-in-law would offer him a job working with the chicken franchise they had become involved in. Things were still good: marital bliss was still the norm in the household and there were no signs of trouble on the horizon. Even where they lived was calm and tranquil—an idyllic slice of the good life. His health was good and permitted him to work fourteen hour days doing a variety of work in the Kentucky Fried Chicken stores because he was given the chance to earn his position as manager first, not gifted the lofty title through nepotism. After a long day at work, he would often go help out with Jaycees, doing everything he could for the club. But it was during these marathon work sessions that his fellow Jaycee members began to catch a glimpse of just how obsessed Gacy was with success and hard work; they saw just how much of a compulsive liar the man was as well.

He would brag about having been "influential politically or of having been appointed to important committees by the governor of Illinois." Every day he tirelessly lied. To top off his intense ambition for work and business, he disturbed others with his need to pathologically lie about how successful and influential he was, to a fault. Another disturbing facet of his personality which cropped up relatively early in people's dealings with Gacy was his desire to drive home the young male employees from the KFC's. Linedecker points out that "the best-looking boys most often got the offers of rides. And not all the boys would accept." What was more disturbing about these refusals were the repercussions of not getting a ride back from John Gacy. If they refused, they knew to stay away from the chicken fryers whenever John was manning them, in case they would fall victim to "accidental" grease burns by his hand. If during this time he was forming his perverse fantasies about the young men he worked with or if he had developed it earlier, it is hard to say, but he certainly was displaying questionable and criminal patterns during his time working with the chicken franchise. Rumors began to spread in his Jaycee community about his homosexuality. Gacy did his due diligence to cover it up and deny any of the accusations, but many had a funny feeling about John regarding his sexual orientation. Given that this was in the 1960's and homosexuality was a very controversial issue, Gacy had a lot of watchful eyes on him. Eventually his actions caught up to him.

One night, Gacy and his wife received a knock on their front door. Upon opening it, they were greeted by a police officer who told them both that Gacy had been indicted for sodomizing a teenage boy. "Producing a search warrant, officers confiscated five rolls of obscene movie film and an envelope containing advertisements for pornographic literature." His wife was disgusted and shocked to find out. Whatever demons that John had had, he certainly did a good job at covering them up: "There had never been anything in their marriage to indicate that her husband harbored a sexual preference for boys." This side of him had never been expressed in any inadvertent way. But there it was, the disturbing details laid before her as she found out that her husband had lured employees of the chicken establishment into her house while she was away with the kids, and had attempted to perform sexual acts, even brandishing a knife during one of the incidents. In that same incident as well, he got the young boy drunk, cut him, choked him, and then sobering up a little bit, let the kid go. His other victims wouldn't be so lucky. He wasn't charged with anything that fit the punishment he deserved just yet though and he denied everything besides partaking in consensual oral sex with a minor.

Despite not facing major legal consequences (at first, but he would be sentenced later) for what he had done and being involved with the young boys, he was still threatened with the prospect of being ostracized from his community and his marriage was in jeopardy as a result. But because he had no prior criminal record and he didn't fit the description of a homosexual, he quickly made the whole incident a case of "being framed." His skills of persuasion and his charm benefitted him once again. But it wasn't enough. During his bid to be president of the Jaycees, the charges loomed over his head and he ultimately lost the election. And the charges just kept piling up for Gacy. What some of his friends had assumed was just a one-time break of the law, mushroomed into a burglary charge, as well as he was found out to have hired an eighteen year-old young man to physically harm one of the boys that had turned him into the grand jury. And those friends of his that may have given him the benefit of the doubt were soon understandably suspicious about his motives and actions. Yet, he still compulsively lied about his involvement with any of the crimes.

He pleaded guilty to the sodomy charge and the other charges were dismissed because he had entered into a plea bargain. But the judge who presided over the case decided that for the safety of any potential teenage boy who would later interact with Gacy, it was imperative for him to be cut off from the general population for ten years. His wife divorced him shortly after. In no time at all, Gacy had lost everything.

Gacy's Time in Prison

Gacy worked just as hard in prison as he had on the outside. If he was anything, he was persistent and able to devote himself wholeheartedly to whatever task he saw fit to accomplish. Survival was number one on his list, of course. He also did a very good job at covering up the real reason he was in jail in the first place. Putting on airs about his hatred for homosexuality, he made a convincing anti-gay figure within prison. He was as persuasive as ever and also made some money with whatever rackets he could manage. He found protection from other inmates and he was making a pretty convincing case that he was capable of changing, that he was going to serve his time and that there wouldn't be any recidivism. And wouldn't you know it, the prison set up their own Jaycee chapter, and Gacy was back in the swing of things, devoting his time to a religious worship of work. He eventually became elected president of the Anamosa Jaycee chapter. Despite losing his wife, freedom, and custody of his kids, at least he had that consolation. Although, he was depressed from losing a respected position in his community for the life of a convict. At that moment, he must have realized that from that point on, if he was going to be involved in the same sort of activity that had landed him in jail, he would have to make sure that his victims couldn't go to the police and rat him out like the ones who had.

And of course, because Gacy had been a model prisoner within the walls of Black Hawk County Jail, he was released on parole after serving just eighteen months in jail. He hadn't gotten into any fights even after he was struck in the face on multiple occasions, he hadn't hung around the wrong crowd, no, he had kept his head down and served his time. Perhaps he was coached or knew it secondhand, but after playacting long enough to keep up appearances and win over the parole board, he was essentially a free man. Linedecker had this to say about his parole, and parole given in general: "No one consulted the judge or prosecutor about the parole. The court's jurisdiction over a felon ends once he or she is sentenced...the convict's immediate fate is in the hands of the Department of Corrections and the Board of Parole." This meant that Gacy only had to win them over and act like a completely changed man for them to grant him the leave that he desired. Having learned that his father had died while he was still in jail, Gacy visited his grave, saddened that he missed him and he never got the chance to repair their relationship. He then moved in with his mother in Chicago.

The Events that Led up to The Crimes

After prison, John began to apply himself to various positions as a cook where he was popular and very skilled at his work. He met Chicago Blackhawk players and made new friends. Prison was quickly becoming ancient history for him; Chicago was his new Mecca. He decided that to best help his recovery and because he wanted some more space to himself after having been an inmate for that stretch of time, that he was ready to own his own house. The neighborhood was a clean, safe to place to live, "the neighbors knew each other, and it was a good safe place to raise children. Parents didn't have to be afraid of letting their children play outside." Within his new house, Gacy immediately got to work on renovating and revamping the existing house. It can be said that he might have been making some sinister adjustments like H.H. Holmes and his castle of horrors. And his new neighbors, they saw him at constant work with fixing and tinkering with the house. He painted the whole house orange as well which drew some concerns from everyone else due to how much the color clashed with the uniform colors of everyone's paintjobs.

After having settled in, it didn't take long for Gacy to return back to his old ways. According to Linedecker, the "Greyhound

Bus Terminal at Clark and Randolph Streets in Chicago's Loop is one of the busiest bus stations in the world. Every day thousands of passengers from cities, towns, and farms throughout the United States and from foreign countries arrive...for some, the trip marks the first time away from the protective arms of parents and friends." And Gacy relied on this fact to pursue the most vulnerable young boys at each bus stop. Gacy was almost charged with forcing a young man to perform sexual acts, but he never showed up in court to cement the sentencing, so Gacy was let off the hook that time. He was still on parole at this time, but because no charges were filed, the board never caught wind of the offense and Gacy was officially released a short time later.

~~~~

He was married again shortly after to one of the neighborhood single moms he had invited over and struck up a friendship with. After a wedding reception, a honeymoon, and many hosted parties over at the Gacy household, his wife and neighbors whom he invited over would start to complain about a musty odor that wafted through the house. Gacy attacked it relentlessly with lime; many neighbors didn't think much of it because they too had heard other residents complain about sewage smells and other curious scents lingering around their house. A hired professional or two and the problem went away though. But for Gacy, the smell was more intense and different. In addition to trying to cover up the curious smell, Gacy also covered up another criminal charge he faced of: "aggravated battery and reckless conduct." Basically, Gacy had impersonated a police officer (as he had done before in Iowa) and had tried to "arrest" a young man. Gacy was not charged with the incident. And, "it would be more than six years before Gacy was again named in a police complaint."
~~~~

After having yet another marriage that was suffering and having confided that he preferred men over women, his relationship with his wife held a bizarre dynamic. She started finding homoerotic pornography around the house, as well as identifications of young boys in Gacy's Oldsmobile, but she kept her lips sealed and carried on with her life without bringing anything up. The strange smell kept persisting in the house. And Gacy, then too old to still be a prominent member of the Jaycee organization, began to help his community with service projects. One of the ways he did this was by inventing a persona which he dubbed "Pogo the Clown." Linedecker says that "his generous stomach provided natural padding to fill out the front, and he topped the baggy suits with a tasseled hat and added oversize shoes and white gloves." His clown work quickly began to spread and he was a very popular addition to birthday groups and other events. He always told others that he was doing far more important events and entertaining large groups of kids in hospitals and such, but these were more tall tales. And Gacy continued to assault and attempt to have his way with young men. Once he was moving along in his contracting business and began hiring fifteen and sixteen year old males to work alongside him, that's when things started escalating as far as disappearances went around the Chicago area.

The Crimes

After having hired a myriad of young men to help with the contracting services, some of those men starting disappearing. It usually coincided with disagreements about payment for the work they did. Linedecker says that Gacy was pretty cheap when it came to actually paying the men for work: "He wasn't as generous with his pay as he was about hosting big parties, loaning his car, and doing favors for neighbors and township Democrats...he paid his young employees only for the time they were actually on the job, even though it might be necessary for them to spend half their time traveling from one work site to another." This would lead to a lot of quarrels over money. Gacy always had work to be done though, especially projects around his house, alone.

Soon, after one disagreement about not getting paid, Johnny Butkovich disappeared. The authorities figured it to be another runaway—those being commonplace for teenagers who would often leave home for a week or so, on borrowed cash, and then would eventually come home without harm. Johnny's situation held a lot of parallels to your typical runaway case. After months had passed and Johnny was still missing, police were less than helpful in finding him. Gacy was questioned as a suspect, but only superficially. Gacy said he had no idea where he was and was sorry he couldn't help them out; he continued with his contracting business unharrassed. His second marriage ended though and this would free up the opportunity to commit as many crimes as he did.

More disappearances happened. What should have been more suspicious was that many of the young men who were disappearing had been involved in Gacy's contracting business and had worked for him. And yet again, the plausible explanation for the disappearances was that they were runaways. This didn't sit well with any of the parents involved. And yet, because multiple disappearances had happened in different police jurisdictions and no communication had been made between officers of different precincts, Gacy wasn't seen as a common link between the disappearances. This isn't to throw the police officers completely under the bus because how likely is it for someone to predict that a crime so sinister could be brewing under their very noses? But there was definitely some negligence that lead to Gacy's being able to get away with what he did. And the numbers kept piling up as boys disappeared that had come into contact with Gacy. Hindsight is so unfortunately clear while the present is often clouded. As Gacy continued his sinister quest, he frequented the male prostitutes of Newtown and assaulted more and more young males. The lengths he was going to were only getting more involved. And it wasn't until the disappearance of Robert Piest that Gacy was finally caught for his crimes.

After being picked up from work, the fifteen-year old Robert Piest was planning on attending a birthday party for his mother. He worked at the pharmacy and was excited to get the celebration started. But first, he had wanted to talk to a man about a contracting job that paid close to double what he was making at the pharmacy. He desperately wanted to make more money as teenagers often do. He went outside of the pharmacy while his mother waited inside and the minutes crept by. Robert wasn't the type of boy to play pranks, dawdle outside, or get caught up in any funny business of the sort; his mother, Elizabeth, started to panic. After driving home, waiting three hours with her husband, they called the police to report that their son was missing. The disappearance tied Gacy to another crime, and this one would stick. Thanks to detective Kozenczak, a thorough investigation was underway because Robert Piest didn't fit the description of your average runaway case. The detective wanted to do his due diligence instead of just write off the runaway as a routine case like many of the detectives had done before.

Because he was the last person to have talked to or seen Robert, Gacy was a prime suspect. In hindsight it seems obvious, but as it has been said multiple times, crimes of this magnitude don't come to mind immediately. He was brought in and questioned. Even though Gacy denied everything, a background check was enough to propel the lead into probable cause territory and a search of his house was in order. On their first search they found many erotic films and paraphernalia, marijuana, a syringe, pills, pictures of drugstores, some stained clothes, handcuffs, knives, driver's licenses of young boys, class rings, and much more. After some lab work and an analysis of hair believed to belong to Robert Piest, a twenty-four-hour surveillance team was organized to watch Gacy's residence in hopes that he would lead them to the boy. He didn't, but the continual pressures of being tailed by cops had put Gacy into such a stressed state that he confessed to the murders of upwards of thirty people to his Attorney. After still tailing Gacy and witnessing him sell marijuana in a very obvious way, possibly as an attempt to cover-up for the more serious crimes he was being scrutinized for, he was eventually detained for the crime when rumors circulated that he had confessed to multiple murders. He was a suicide and flight risk, so any charges they could slap on him would keep him immobile while they attempted to pin him to various crimes. It didn't work.

They began telling him that they were going to be ripping up floorboards and check the crawlspace, and in a panic, "Gacy blurted out that he had killed a man in self-defense. But it wouldn't be necessary to rip up the floorboards of the house to find him. Gacy said he had buried the body under his garage and offered to show detectives the locations of the makeshift grave." The policemen knew without a doubt that they had found the man responsible for killing many individuals. They sent police officers over to his residence immediately and searched the crawlspace and underneath the floorboards. They found multiple bodies there, underneath the house, and it didn't take long for Gacy to just go ahead and confess. He knew he had been found out, and he didn't want to run any longer. The evidence they had found was damning.

In order to make sure that the crime scene was preserved as best as they could, the whole site was treated with the delicateness of an archaeological dig site. Five of the bodies of his victims were dumped in the Des Plaines River. Gacy was then formally charged with the murder of Robert Piest. He then cooperated in telling the police officers where exactly he buried all of the bodies, drawing a diagram that showed the dimensions of his house and helping them quickly know where they were buried. Confirming many of the details that Gacy gave were the souvenirs of his victims that he kept, often in the form of identification or clothing that would point towards the identity of whomever he had killed. The subsequent days after Gacy had been detained and had confessed were spent digging up his property, looking for bodies. Gacy had been telling the truth and had provided a very accurate map of where his victims were. Many of them were covered in lime because it hastened decomposition. Almost all of the bodies were arranged in the way that he had described. Gacy was methodical and compulsive. The amateur clown enthusiast, businessman, cook, pathological liar, and family man had harbored a secret identity that was atrocious in scope.

After the bodies were exhumed, Linedecker said that "John Gacy had now been linked to more murders than any other individual in the history of the United States." And that accolade clearly meant something to his perverse brain because "shortly after his arrival at the county jail complex, he began collecting articles about himself from newspapers and magazines, which he filed in a folder." As if he was proud that he had eclipsed the worse confirmed serial killers in history or that he had gotten away with it for so long. Many years later, in 1994, John Wayne Gacy was put to death by lethal injection. And thus ended his life.

Made in United States
Troutdale, OR
06/30/2024